"Rick Hopkins is a man on a mission, a mission to help people see that "Non-Profit" does not mean "No-Profit!" He shares incredible ideas to help people to learn how to create nonprofit organizations that do good, while doing well. This book explores the truth behind the long standing rumor that nonprofits must consign themselves to an existence based on scarcity rather than abundance. Excellent nonprofits are capable of building the necessary financial infrastructure to, not only survive tough economic times, but to thrive in them. I highly recommend this book for people in non-profit arena as well as people in the profit arena. It is a powerful book!"

–Willie Jolley- Best Selling Author of "A Setback Is A Setup For A Comeback" and "An Attitude of Excellence!"

"WOW, I simply love this book. Seldom does a book say it better or more powerfully than Nonprofit Doesn't Mean No Profit. This book is a must read for those want to navigate the slippery slope of a changing economy and its impact on the incredible world of nonprofits. My heartfelt thanks goes out to Rick Hopkins for giving us this well researched, thought out and timely gem."

–George C. Fraser, Author, "Success Runs In Our Race" and "Click"

"Generating resources is critical to any not-for-profit organization because you can only do as much good as you can afford. Rick has been able to accurately articulate some key principles that translate into tremendous revenue generating opportunities for not-for-profit organizations."

–Eric K. Mann, President and CEO, YMCA of Florida's First Coast

D0808124

"*The nonprofit sector is too important an economic and workforce engine – and has too much potential for growth and innovation – to be defeated by the temporary economic challenges that we currently face and that lay ahead. Any book that will assist us in developing an economic road map for sustainability of the nonprofit industry is a "must read."*

–Diane Bell McKoy, President and CEO, Associated Black Charities

"*In today's economic world we can be sure that nothing is certain and many things that have been the norm will certainly pass away due to lack of creativity and vision. Therefore, our nonprofit community must realize that flexibility is essential to success and creativity is the backbone of business longevity. In this book, Rick challenges nonprofits to become divergent thinkers who aggressively seek out and implement new paradigms for financial sustainability*"

–James Dula, PhD, Public Administrator

Nonprofit
DOESN'T MEAN
NO *Profit*

To Joe,

Thanks for your
Support

7/15/12

Nonprofit DOESN'T MEAN NO Profit

A **FINANCIAL SUCCESS STRATEGY** FOR THE NEW ECONOMY

G.M. "RICK" HOPKINS

— TABLE OF CONTENTS —

Nonprofit DOESN'T MEAN NO Profit

This book, *Nonprofit Doesn't Mean No Profit,* will challenge nonprofit organizations to consider a new paradigm for economic sustainability. They must find opportunity in the challenges presented by this recession, rather than be paralyzed by it. In tough economic times, it has always been the creative and the innovative who have provided the spark that leads to economic recovery. Throughout the book, you will be exposed to new ways of looking at old challenges that, hopefully, will open your eyes to new ideas for making your nonprofit organization sustainable in the toughest economic times.

ABOUT THE AUTHOR

 Rick Hopkins is president of G.M. Hopkins & Associates, Inc., a Washington, DC area nonprofit consulting firm specializing in fundraising, board development and fiscal management. He is retired from a thirty year career as a senior executive for the national YMCA movement where he produced millions of dollars annually in membership, program and fundraising revenue. An outstanding operator and fundraiser, Hopkins passed along these skills to over a dozen mentees who later became top level executives in the nonprofit industry.

— CHAPTER ONE —

The Rumor Isn't True

That's right, the rumor isn't true… nonprofits _ARE_ supposed to make a profit! Part of the misunderstanding comes from improper use of the colloquial term "**nonprofit.**" Merriam-Webster defines "colloquial" as a statement "…of or relating to conversation…" or "…used in or characteristic of familiar and informal conversation; unacceptably informal." In other words, if you use a word enough times in such a way that people come to understand it in that context; then you have, in fact, created a new word. The proper term is "**not-for-profit.**" This is more accurate because it speaks to the reason why the organization was created… or in this case NOT created. A nonprofit organization is not created with the predominant purpose being to make money; but this does not imply that making money is not necessary for the organization to endure.

"**For-profit**" companies and businesses were created to make money... plain and simple. They make no excuses for that, and should not have to. For profit businesses are the backbone of our capitalistic society. The for-profit's primary purpose is to generate profit. The nonprofit's primary purpose is to serve the community. It is not the ability to generate profit, or lack thereof, that determines for-profit or nonprofit status... it is what is *done* with the profit that differentiates the two. This fundamental difference in the purpose of the entity is the core principle that guides the actions of each.

> **FOR-PROFIT:** These are companies that distribute their profits to the shareholders, boards and staff in the form of shares of stock, dividends, and bonuses. They may be privately or publicly owned.

> **NONPROFIT OR NOT-FOR-PROFIT:** These are organizations that reinvest their profits back into the organization and the community. Nonprofits are publicly owned. They may apply for, and receive, tax-exempt status from the federal government. 501(c)(3) organizations are the most common category of tax-exempt organization. We call them nonprofits because it's easier, not because it is accurate. In my mind, the term nonprofit does have a specific meaning: it means "out of business!"

That explanation provides background to the vicious rumor that nonprofit organizations are not supposed to make a profit. This mistruth has since grown to epic proportions and done a lot of damage along the way. Today, many community organizations operate under the umbrella of that assumption; perpetuating the myth that being on the verge of financial ruin is normal. These organizations unwittingly reinforce the false notion that being in the red is an expected side effect of running a nonprofit. In the eyes of some, teetering on the edge of financial ruin is somehow evidence that an organization is doing good work. Not only is this a silly myth—it is a dangerous one. Just as in traffic, when you see red on the map of your financial forecast, you need to stop what you're doing and truly think about where your organization is headed

> "Among signs of fiscal stress, about half of responding organizations have cash reserves for less than three months' of operating expenses or say they are over reliant on a limited number of funders (48 percent each). This analysis suggests that in the United States, large numbers of nonprofit, charitable organizations—and particularly the smaller entities...—are struggling to secure funding for the vital services they provide in their communities."
>
> —"Late Fall 2011 Nonprofit Fundraising Study", December 2011, Nonprofit Research Collaborative

NO MARGIN... NO MISSION

In the real world, *any company, business, organization or agency that does not make a profit will soon be out of business.* Period. There *is* a business side to the nonprofit world. Fee-for-service is not the singular domain of for-profit companies and businesses. Take hospitals, for example. Nonprofit hospitals can provide the same level of quality care and service as their for-profit counterparts; and can justify charging market rates for their efforts. YMCAs can provide health and wellness facilities equal to any for-profit health club or fitness center; and some of the best camping and child care programs are run by churches, Boys & Girls Clubs, and the Salvation Army.

For most nonprofits, however, fee-for-service is not a primary revenue generator. It is for these nonprofits, in particular, that the following guideline applies:

A nonprofit has two sides: a charity side and a business side. Be sure to run the charity like a charity, and the business like a business. If you run the charity like a business and the business like a charity … you will soon be out of business!

So how does a nonprofit that lacks significant fee-for-service capability still operate in a fiscally sound manner that may, ultimately, allow them to generate a profit? It is essential that every nonprofit gain control of three often overlooked business-side operational areas:

1. **Overhead Costs** consist of human resource expenses like staff salaries, taxes and benefits.

2. **Occupancy Costs** are necessities such as: rent/mortgage payments, utility bills, insurance, and facility and grounds maintenance.

3. **Indirect Costs** are any hidden expenses that do not fit within the other two categories (i.e., the prizes you

have to buy for the raffle when in-kind donations fall short).

These costs may seem trivial compared to your primary goal of providing services, but underestimating these expenses can have disastrous consequences on the overall organization. The charity can't run if the building is falling down. While it may be tempting simply to rely on the portion of fundraising already allocated for these costs, emergencies do happen. Just as in day-to-day life, a single calamity—that collapsed roof or a small fire—can easily wipe out a small budget. While this may be a difficult concept for staunch traditionalists to grasp, the times dictate that we now consider non-traditional, out of the box options to bring in funds for basic needs that may, in fact, have nothing to do with your nonprofit's mission or services offered. In a down economic climate, you don't want to be at risk of closing your doors simply because you haven't received as many donations as expected, or you fall short in another of the "old dependable" revenue streams.

> *"One of the important findings of the Nonprofit Overhead Cost Project is that overhead, far from a 'necessary evil,' is the basis for mission effectiveness."*
> **–"Lessons for Boards from the Nonprofit Overhead Cost Project", The Urban Institute and Indiana University**

Fair warning, as you seek to make the transition from "just-hanging-on" to "financially profitable", it won't be an easy switch. Even if you are eager to start a new path you may have to drag others along, kicking and screaming every step of the way. Remember, the world has established assumptions of how a nonprofit should function that may clash with your new determination of what *your* nonprofit needs to do and be in order to survive. Remember, you can't do business if you are out of business.

Example:

> The director of a nonprofit is looking for ways to help the budget and decides to rent conference rooms to community groups. A space/cost analysis confirms that $75 per hour is the appropriate rental fee based on comparable venues in the area. A community group inquires about renting a conference room for its next board meeting, but balks at the $75 an hour rate. "You should be ashamed of yourself," they tell the director. "You are supposed to be a non-profit. You are supposed to help the community; not try to make a profit from us."

LET'S MAKE A DEAL

Would that same person argue with a grocery store manager over the price of a can of peas? Would that person attempt to guilt, coerce, or otherwise emotionally blackmail any *for*-profit business professional in this manner? This person's response has a lot to do with the world's perception of what a nonprofit represents. Certainly, giving is the primary purpose of every nonprofit, but staying in business is necessary to that goal.

The key to understanding the needs of a properly functioning nonprofit is the ability to define the foundation of balance, and, from a fiscal management standpoint, go beyond to find a positive *imbalance.*

In determining how to define the foundation of balance, just think of the Yin-and-Yang in Eastern philosophy or the law of physics – that every action has an equal and opposite reaction. In business there are balancing equations, as well. Business accounting requires that every credit be balanced by a debit, but imbalances are common. In the world of nonprofit, an organization that earns more than it spends has a **surplus**. More often, organizations spend more than they earn, resulting in **deficit**.

Once a nonprofit goes into deficit, the initial panic may prompt immediate, disastrous reactions. Many nonprofits will immediately cut into overhead human resource costs by reducing staff. While this seems to make sense, unlike for-profit businesses, nonprofit staff are normally overworked and underpaid from the start. Cutting one nonprofit employee can be more like cutting two or three for-profit employees, who generally have more specific and defined duties than their nonprofit counterparts. The savings in cost will often pale in comparison to the sudden loss of manpower and experience.

> "While the economy is slowly recovering, the nonprofit sector has not seen improvement in fundraising results yet. What improvements are occurring appear to benefit the larger nonprofit organizations. ... The smallest organizations, in particular, are feeling many signs of fiscal stress. In response, a larger share of these charities are reducing staff and struggling to find ways to raise revenue. These factors are likely to affect the availability and quality of services in communities around the country in 2012."
>
> —"Late Fall 2011 Nonprofit Fundraising Study", December 2011, Nonprofit Research Collaborative

The initial response of nonprofits to cut spending when they find themselves in negative imbalance is counterproductive because nonprofits rarely overspend. Most of these organizations find themselves in deficit because they are not generating enough revenue. Therefore, it is imperative that a nonprofit seek out ways to bring in revenue so they are never forced to cut into necessary costs. In this way, the organization has identified the foundation of balance necessary to sustain and proceeded to go beyond by identifying additional forms of revenue to create a positive imbalance they can be happy with. Remember: nonprofits seldom have expense problems... they have revenue problems!

> *"In general, nonprofits are becoming more businesslike. Economic and political pressures are requiring them to operate as efficiently as possible. Nonprofits are setting more stringent financial goals, discussing strategic planning, and repositioning themselves to take advantage of market niches."*
> —**"Careers in Nonprofit Organizations", Career Development Series Guide, Miami University**

Let's put the rumor to rest.

An organization that truly gives everything will never have enough to give back to the community. To quote the sage, Dr. Phil: "You teach others how to treat you." I suggest, that doesn't just apply to people. Run the business side of your organization with financial health in mind and you will teach the community to respect and appreciate your organization. There is no need to publicize, explain, or ask permission to shed the burden of the myth. Many good organizations have burned themselves out trying to live under that impossible standard. Today, make the decision to join the minority of nonprofits that have embraced the right to be financially sound and, yes, even make a profit. Remember, it is the job of the nonprofit to educate by example and let financial stability be its best evidence of its commitment to serve. It is not enough simply to survive. The nonprofit must use techniques of excellence to strive for the positive imbalance called profit.

This is just good business.

NOTES

— CHAPTER TWO —

Strive for Greatness

MAKING THE DECISION

In order to strive for profit, a nonprofit must first strive for greatness.

Early in my career, I was Executive Director of a small inner city YMCA in Richmond, Virginia. I remember speaking at a monthly meeting of our corporate-sponsored mentor program for urban youth. These were not just your average group of high school students. They were the cream of the crop, academically; many of them would later attend college on academic scholarships. The topic of careers came up. I asked the aspiring future professionals, who among them wanted to be a doctor, a lawyer, or an engineer, someday? Almost everyone raised their hand for one of the three choices. I then asked:

"Who would like to be a nonprofit executive, someday?" **Not a single hand.** It appears the myth was alive and well amongst these young adults. I was not surprised; but I was a little hurt and disappointed and saw this overwhelming aversion to my chosen profession as a little bit of a slap in the face. As comedian Rodney Dangerfield might have said: "We don't get no respect... no respect at all!"

The group apparently believed that a medical degree, in and of itself, would make them successful... whatever that meant to them. In reality, neither a law or engineering degree would stand any better chance of accomplishing this objective; nor would an MBA or Ph.D. So, what about these particular careers was so appealing to these young people as opposed to being a nonprofit executive. Of course, I asked them that very question, and their answer should not surprise you... it was the money! They saw those professions as being imminently profitable and, to them, represented excellence. Very little thought seemed to have been given to whether or not they actually liked the work. After all, if the money was good then the work had to be satisfying as well, right? Sure, any one of these kids could become a doctor or lawyer or engineer, but it seemed they were so caught up in the titles and perceived wealth that they failed to understand it didn't really matter which profession they went into... only *excellence* would determine how far they went.

By the way, my wife, at the time, was an electrical engineer at a Fortune 500 company headquartered in the area. They thought I was lying when I told them that, as a nonprofit executive, I made more money than she did. Their paradigm could not accept it. They believed that nonprofit organizations always lost money and that nonprofit executives could not possibly make a six-figure salary. If nonprofits do not work hard to dispel the misconception that nonprofit agencies will always be fiscally irresponsible, and that a professional career in the industry can only be financially unrewarding; we will not be able to attract the top young talent that we need to secure a sustainable future.

> "Typically, individuals seeking a career in the nonprofit sector know that this is not the type of career that provides a millionaire's salary. However, it is a misconception that people in the nonprofit sector cannot make ends meet. In fact, some statistics indicate that in certain sub-sectors of the economy, nonprofit workers are paid better than their for-profit counterparts."
> **–"Careers in Nonprofit Organizations", Career Development Series Guide, Miami University**

EXCELLENCE IS AS EXCELLENCE DOES

The for-profit industry, generally speaking, seems to feel a sense of false superiority towards nonprofits in the business arena. However, even more damaging is the unfortunate fact that many nonprofits also feel that same way about themselves. When compared to excellent for profit CEOs, excellent nonprofit CEOs actually function at a higher level of leadership due to their ability to get more out of less using noncompensatory means. Monetary compensation and financial reward still drive the for profit economic engine. The nonprofit CEO must rely on a higher level of leadership skill based on relationships and intrinsic motivation. I wish I had a dollar for every volunteer who joined a nonprofit board with the intent of "saving" the organization with pearls of wisdom gleaned from their many years of experience in the "real world." There is no doubt that nonprofits have much to learn from their for-profit counterparts; but the converse is also true. For-profits have an awful lot they can learn from nonprofits as well… whether they choose to acknowledge it or not.

In his outstanding book, *Good to Great and the Social Sectors*, author Jim Collins writes: "We must reject the idea—well-intentioned, but dead wrong—that the primary path to greatness in the social sectors is to become more like a business. Most businesses, like most anything else in life, fall somewhere between mediocre and good. Few are great. Many widely practiced business norms correlate with mediocrity, not greatness. So why would we want to import the practices of mediocrity into the social sectors?"

I concur, wholeheartedly. **In fact, great businesses have more in common with great nonprofits than they do with other mediocre businesses!** Therefore, it is the pursuit of greatness itself, not of a particular discipline, that should be the ultimate goal of for-profits and nonprofits, alike. It is the same for young people when planning their futures. Excellence should be the goal, no matter the career choice. It has been proven time and again that what gets measured gets done. Excellent for-profits excel at performance measurement and business metrics and have a clear advantage here; even mediocre for-profits tend to do a decent job with business metrics. This is not to say that excellent nonprofits do not measure; but they tend to be the exception in the industry. Nonprofits, when they do so, tend to measure non-financial metrics; which are inherently much more difficult to quantify. For profits personify the belief that "if it doesn't make dollars, it doesn't make sense." Nonprofits may do well to incorporate this as well, to the extent that it is compatible with their charitable mission, of course.

My point all along has been that nonprofits need to focus equally as hard on financial metrics as they do on more subjective ones. Ironically, great success in charitable, mission-driven initiatives often does not translate into financial reward commensurate with providing ongoing sustainability for the organization. In other words, "warm and fuzzy" may feel good, but it doesn't feed the bulldog.

"The nonprofit industry conjures images of altruistic workers who forgo private-sector lucre for the good of society. The reality, though, is that many nonprofits are large, sophisticated organizations that pay well to lure executives who might otherwise move to for-profit companies."
—"Hundreds of Employees at Nonprofits Make Six-Figure Salaries", Jeff Ostrowski, Pam Beach Post Online, December 2011

HOW DO YOU LIKE ME NOW?

More than anything else, this chapter is about making nonprofit organizations and staff feel good about themselves, acknowledging their worth and their special gifts. Let us not make the same mistake that others make when evaluating our capacity for greatness. Not everyone could do what nonprofit professionals do. The hardest part about being a nonprofit executive is that, for some reason, other people seem to inherently believe that they can do our jobs better than we can. They just don't think it is that tough... but they are wrong! Let me give an example from my past.

Many years ago I was a regional vice president with a large metropolitan area YMCA. We recruited another regional VP from one of the top for profit health clubs in the area. She caught on to what we did very quickly and years later was promoted to chief operating officer. Soon after she arrived, however, a few branch director vacancies became available. Our new VP had not been on board long, so she was not yet aware of all that a YMCA branch director actually did. One day she said to me, "let me make a few phone calls, I know several people who ran clubs for me at my old job that could fill those vacancies right now." For brevity's sake I will fast forward a few months. That same VP later came to me and said, "I'm glad I didn't recruit those club managers from my old job. They couldn't have cut it."

What changed her mind? She now understood that a YMCA branch director did much more than just manage a fitness facility, sell memberships and provide good customer service. He also had to recruit and give leadership to a volunteer board and committees, run an annual fundraising campaign and put on special events. Additionally, he had to operate state licensed preschool, after school child care and summer day camp programs. Many facilities also had swimming pools which was just one more high risk venue that had to be managed.

Was I successful? Did I make you feel good about yourself and what you do? I hope so, because the next few chapters will challenge you to look at what you do differently. It will challenge your ideas about fiscal responsibility, and about "the good, the bad and the ugly" of making money. Hang in there with me. I will get to the traditional stuff toward the end. Please don't peek!

NOTES

— CHAPTER THREE —

Excellence Through Entrepreneurship

CATCH THE SPIRIT

The severe economic downturn affecting this country over the last few years has forced all economic sectors, especially nonprofits, to look at finances differently. In the final analysis, nonprofits are no different than for-profits or private individuals when it comes down to economic survival. All have been hit hard and must think and act outside the box in order to survive. Ironically, great fortunes have been made during the toughest economic times by those creative and resourceful enough to see opportunities invisible to the masses; and then act upon them. We call these innovators *Entrepreneurs*. They are sometimes borne of necessity but always utilize creativity; allowing them to think beyond the confines of what is "normal". We call this thinking and acting outside the box.

There are reasons why the entrepreneurial spirit is especially important in the nonprofit industry. Once again, those myths we mentioned earlier filter down into the details when it comes to running a nonprofit. And as we already noted, if all nonprofits stay "within the box" in terms of mindset, many of them will fail. Statistics tell us that many have failed. Just as nonprofits have been misled to believe that they should not make a profit, they been misled to assume the spirit of American charity will always see them through.

Let's look at the collection of operating assumptions that could hinder a nonprofit:

MYTH: Americans are the most generous and charitable people on earth. Americans will always dig deep into their pockets in support of a worthy cause or deserving organization.

IN THE REAL WORLD...

There is no shortage of worthy causes today, and during lean economic times people are forced to make difficult choices with their charitable dollars. Unfortunately, some nonprofits find out the hard way that there just isn't enough charity to go around.

MYTH: Government grants are always available and plentiful if the need is obvious and your cause is compelling.

IN THE REAL WORLD...

The government also cuts back on giving in the midst of a poor economic climate. The following quote is in relation to our most recent downturn, and in reference to the release of a national study by the Urban Institute on the subsequent effect on nonprofits...

> *"Many human-service groups are slicing services to those in need in the face of widespread cuts in government support ... declines in government funds—along with reductions in contributions and investment income—have led to a 'hollowing of organizational capacity that may take years to rebuild, if ever,' as many of these agencies have had to scale back their operations. As a result, they are cutting back services like food, job training, and child care even as demand for these services is on the rise."*
>
> **–"As Government Money Dwindles, Many Human-Service Groups Cut Back Assistance to the Needy", Grant Williams, The Chronicle of Philanthropy, October, 2010**

MYTH: Any holes not filled with public funding could be filled by grants and donations from foundations and corporate sponsors.

IN THE REAL WORLD...

Foundations and corporate sponsors are also affected by the economic climate. Just as we all cut back when times get tight, "cutting back" for a foundation may mean cutting your organization's funding needs from their budget.

MYTH: No need to worry about grassroots fundraising and annual support campaigns. Sure, the occasional special event is fine; but there is no need to incorporate the participants into the annual campaign structure as volunteers and donors. People don't want to be bothered, and besides, that is too much work.

IN THE REAL WORLD...

Nonprofits rely on—and thrive with—strong volunteer staffs.

> *"More than two million people lost jobs in 2008, and many talented and experienced managers have time on their hands. If they started volunteering, they could help many nonprofits navigate the next couple of years."*
> **–"Can Volunteers Be a Lifeline for Nonprofit Groups?",**
> **Kelley Holland, The New York Times Online, January 2009**

MYTH: Nonprofit board members are too busy with their "real jobs" to be bothered with making personal donations, raising money in the annual campaign and volunteering to work special events.

IN THE REAL WORLD...

Those tasks are precisely what a board should be doing. It is the board's job to raise funds in a manner and timeline consistent with the needs and purpose of the organization.

> "A good board member is someone who is interested in the organization's purpose, willing to work within a group, and be in a position to make financial contributions to the organization, or to find others who will."
>
> —"Establishing a Nonprofit Organization", The Foundation Center

We would all love to believe that where there is a need there will always be a donor to fill it, but you don't want to bet your organization's future on the hope that someone, somehow, will be able and willing to bail you out when times get tough. Even if you start on firm ground, a shift in the national economic climate can destroy your plans for your organization, simply because it has altered the plans of your donors. So much for the imaginary security blanket you've depended on to get your organization through the tough times.

Maybe you didn't need me to spell out the ramifications as I've done. Maybe you've seen the results of this way of operating first-hand. How many nonprofits do you know of that had to close their doors, or significantly cut back on their programs and services due to loss of grant funding? Over-dependence on single source funding is the kiss of death for any business… nonprofits are no exception.

Or … maybe yours *is* the organization that has been following all the rules and feels to do otherwise would betray that unspoken mandate; that caring about the financial viability of your nonprofit is somehow a sign of your lack of dedication to your community. If you are a nonprofit that has faithfully ascribed to those myths, I have only one question:

HOW IS THAT WORKING FOR YOU?

At this point, there is no use in regret over the manner with which you've run your organization in the past. It's time to start fresh, casting off the traditional rules that will keep you chained to "just barely making it"-status. Nonprofits that are presently struggling to survive should adopt a new paradigm for a new economy... a paradigm based on *entrepreneurship*!

The spirit of entrepreneurship is one of the things that makes America great. Its people always seem to find a way to make lemons into lemonade. In my experience, the best example of this entrepreneurial spirit occurred in Rochester, NY in the mid-1990s. The "Big 3" major employers—Kodak, Xerox and Bausch & Lomb—went through extensive layoffs, simultaneously. The experts predicted the economy was surely doomed. Fast forward several months. To the surprise of many, the economy did not collapse. It held steady and over time, actually grew! How was this possible? An unexpected massive surge in entrepreneurship saved the day. Fortunately, most of the people laid off were educated, seasoned, skilled employees. A large number of them chose to forego the "cycle of pain" involving sending out hundreds of resumes, collecting unemployment, or becoming wards of the welfare state. They simply started their own successful businesses using the knowledge and experience gained while they were employees. Some were even able to hire back many of their former Big 3 co-workers.

I don't mean to imply that this was a typical situation. After all, Rochester was a highly educated white-collar town with options unavailable to many communities. I only hold it up as an example of what true entrepreneurial spirit can accomplish.

Admittedly, it will be difficult for many nonprofits to adopt this entrepreneurial spirit if they've never tapped into it before, but no more difficult than it would be for the majority of individuals. We were raised from birth to be employees, not business owners. We were raised to be consumers, not producers. The philosophies and attitudes of the Industrial Age reinforced this mindset. While it is true that entrepreneurship flourishes during tough economic times, it seldom takes the exact same form. It only makes sense that entrepreneurship born at the time of the information age and global economy of the early 21st Century would differ from entrepreneurship during the aftermath of the Great Depression and Industrial Age. The choice is yours. You can wait for the economy to get even worse or you can act. Nonprofits *must* embrace the spirit of entrepreneurship; they must fully utilize their resourcefulness and creativity toward finding ways to generate enough revenue to grow and sustain their organization by whatever means necessary.

NOTES

— CHAPTER FOUR —

Moving Entrepreneurism to Action

WE ARE NOT IN KANSAS ANYMORE

Once nonprofits embrace entrepreneurism, they gain a powerful economic weapon against current and future recessionary times. With the wide-spread utilization of the internet and social media, the ability to brand, market, advertise and promote products and services has placed tremendous economic power squarely in the hands of entrepreneurial-minded individuals and organizations. The predominant media tools of the past—TV, radio and print advertising—no longer dominate. In fact, fewer people today are watching TV, listening to radio or reading newspapers and magazines. Let me be clear. People are still watching a screen, but now it is a computer or smart phone screen. They are still listening to music and broadcasts; but laptops, I-Pods© and those doggone smart phones have replaced radio as the platform of choice. I did not mean to leave the impression that people no longer read newspapers, books and magazines... they are simply reading them on their portable and hand-held electronic devices.

So what opportunities does this epiphany present for nonprofits? Our capitalistic society is fueled by advertising dollars. The redistribution of those advertising dollars represents a tremendous opportunity for nonprofits to capitalize on new sources of leveraged residual income to fund its organizational infrastructure. Where am I going with this? Bear with me a while longer while we "follow the money". Let's start with the plight of the for-profit businesses, companies and corporations. With less revenue to work with, major companies can no longer afford massive amounts of expensive TV and other traditional advertising media. Large marketing and advertising departments can no longer be justified... neither can large sales forces. Bring on the pink slips!

How does this help nonprofits? With large companies no longer able to market and advertise their products and services in the traditional manner, they have had to turn to the way they used to do it back in the "good old days;" by using non-employee, independent contractors to market directly to their personal and professional networks. Where do they get the money to pay these independent contractors? Simple... it comes from advertising dollars that companies *used* to spend on TV, radio and print ads! This methodology goes by many names. Whether you call it network marketing, direct sales, relationship marketing, direct distribution, etc.; combined with the internet and social media financial experts like Warren Buffet and Robert Kiyosaki believe it represents the greatest opportunity in history for everyday people to strengthen their bottom lines. They believe this so strongly that they now own network marketing companies themselves. I see this same opportunity for nonprofits to leverage other companies' products and services with minimal start-up cost, recurring operating costs and legal encumbrances. In many ways, the network marketing model reminds me of the traditional nonprofit fundraising pyramid model. The great majority of donations come from many people making small gifts. These small gifts make up the very foundation of the fundraising effort. You need a few "heavy hitters" to get the ball rolling, and some solid contributors in the middle; but it is the foundation of many small donors that give year after year and provide stability and sustainability to the nonprofit organization.

WHERE EVERYBODY KNOWS YOUR NAME

I see yet another parallel between traditional nonprofit fundraising methodologies and that of the network marketing industry. They are both built on relationships. Nonprofits call it "friend-raising;" network marketers call it "recruiting." Subtle differences notwithstanding, the end result can ultimately be the same. Always keep in mind that one's opinion, no matter how biased or enlightened, is merely a product of point of view. As such, it was this close relationship between relationship building and success shared by both disciplines that caused me to see the great potential for nonprofits to easily adapt a skill they were already experts at (fundraising) to one which allowed them to generated unlimited amounts of leveraged residual income with minimal risk marketing and distributing other companies' products and services. One of the biggest complaints nonprofits have about donated income is that it is often severely restricted as to its allowed usage. This is a good thing. It encourages due diligence and discourages fraud. However, if you remember nothing else from this book, remember that "an earned dollar is an unrestricted dollar." If your nonprofit is struggling to meet payroll or to pay its utilities or to repair its physical plant… it is absolutely okay to use earned revenue to do this! You own it. You control it. It doesn't expire in a couple of years, get cut back due to government or foundation shortfalls, and is not limited only to people who support your charitable mission.

The brutal fact is that there are infinitely more people who, regardless of what you do, will NOT write a check to support your cause than WILL. Why not let those people still help fund your operations by purchasing products and services through non-traditional revenue generating ventures. Think of money as energy. It cannot be destroyed; it merely changes forms. Nonprofits need to be able to recognize money in its many forms, the opportunities to create it and the opportunities to act upon it.

Many of you purchased this book expecting to learn more about fundraising and board development... and you will. Hang in there with me for one more chapter, then, I promise, we will roll up our sleeves and dive head-first into my own version of traditional fundraising and board development. While I may seem to be quite open to new ways of operating nonprofit organizations, I was not always so. I am a staunch traditionalist when it comes to fundraising... but I am also a realist. But more than anything else, I recognize the importance of survival over ideology; that if you are out of business you can do nothing to help your community.

FOUR WALLS VERSUS NO WALLS

So, how does a nonprofit go about selecting a nontraditional revenue stream? Before I answer that, I want you to take stock of what is happening around you.

Look at what happened with Blockbuster Video and Barnes & Noble Book Stores. I have been a loyal, card-carrying Blockbuster member for as long as I can remember. As I traveled around the country, there always seemed to be a Blockbuster store nearby where I could stop in and rent all the movies that my workaholic lifestyle caused me to miss at the theatre. A few years ago, the store in my neighborhood closed. No problem, I thought, there was also one near where I worked. Within months, that one closed. I was left with one last chance. Not far from one of the field operations I supervised was yet another Blockbuster Video Store. Unfortunately, within a year, that one closed as well. What happened? Can you say "Netflix?"

Blockbuster built its business based on a "Four Walls Strategy." The four walls strategy requires a physical building and all the associated overhead costs such as: staffing, rent, utilities, facility maintenance, insurance and other occupancy costs. Netflix wisely chose a "No Walls Strategy." They decided not to invest in physical plants that were expensive to maintain and operate; instead, they chose to use the internet to sell and rent videos from the warehouse and ship them directly to the consumers' mailbox. They also were able to make the seamless transition to digital transmission of their products and services through our personal and handheld mobile devices, further solidifying their position.

Amazon is another example of flawless execution of the no walls strategy. One of my favorite things to do during my down time was to go to my local Barnes and Noble Bookstore, buy a book or magazine, then go to the Café to sit and enjoy a cup of coffee and a pastry while reading and relaxing. Apparently, like the dinosaurs, people like me are who prefer to go someplace and do something there about to become extinct. It seems that Amazon figured out many more people would prefer to shop for books and magazines online and drink their own coffee at home. Perhaps it is a product of the recessionary economy, or the high price of gasoline, or lack of free time… or all of the above. It wasn't long before my favorite Barnes & Noble Book Store went the same route as my favorite Blockbuster Video Store. I was forced to come along, kicking and screaming, into the 21st Century where I now rent my videos and buy my books online. It is undeniable that the world is now online and if I want to stay connected, I need to bring more aspects of my personal and professional life online as well.

Soon to become extinct is the bank drive-up teller window. This will be my last great act of defiance. As long as there is an actual person at the teller window, I will continue to go to that window... even if the line is longer or all I want is a simple account balance. However, even a dinosaur like me can see what is coming... and I would be foolish not to prepare for it. Forewarned is forearmed. My point is this: nonprofits should proactively look for new revenue streams that embrace the no walls philosophy. By now, the reason should be obvious. Don't be a dinosaur!

IT'S THE ECONOMY, STUPID

After retirement, I started my own nonprofit consulting company: **G.M. Hopkins & Associates, Inc**. I was confident that my expertise in fundraising, board development, strategic planning and fiscal management would enable me to handsomely supplement my pension by sharing my knowledge with struggling nonprofits in a consulting capacity. Unfortunately, my timing could not have been worse. The nation's economy went into the worst tailspin since the Great Depression. As hard as for-profits and individuals were hit by the recession, nonprofits were hit even harder. They simply could not afford to pay for much-needed consulting services, except in the areas of fundraising and special events. By focusing on providing primarily fundraising support, I was able to peddle my wares to a few small nonprofits, agreeing to take my compensation out of the "back end" from money I had helped them raise. As expected, I found that before I could even begin to help my new employers, these organizations first needed to define and implement basic internal practices and procedures upon which to build an effective fundraising campaign. Realistically, this would take more time than either of us had to make this happen.

> "But there's more to a good consultant than knowing the body of knowledge in fund development. You need an organizational development specialist. Why? Because most fundraising problems are _not_ fundraising problems. They are problems in other parts of your organization."
> —"Should You Hire a Fundraising Consultant? I Don't Know – and I am One!", Simone Joyaux, The Nonprofit Quarterly, Online, February 2011

An old Native American proverb states that "In darkest night, bright stars are revealed." Fortunately, this was also the time of mass energy deregulation in several states across America. I stumbled upon an energy company that was using the network marketing model to attract customers. This energy company was introducing a new FREE fundraising program for nonprofits. Enrollment was also free for supporters of the nonprofit, and as a bonus they also received a 10% to 20% discount on their monthly electric and gas service. But most importantly, the energy company paid the nonprofit (and me!) every time a supporter paid his/her utility bill for as long as the supporter remained a customer. It was a win-win scenario that enabled the nonprofit to make significant money without having to sell donuts, pizza or bottled water on street corners, and it paid *me* because I sponsored the nonprofit into the program. That was merely the first of many examples where I have seen nonprofits take control of their fiscal situation through finding a nontraditional alternative to generate much-needed operational income. As more and more large companies have changed their marketing, advertising and distribution models from traditional to direct sales, an amazing array of products and services are now available. This presents a wide range of opportunities for almost any nonprofit to find a product or service that fits comfortably into its organization's stated purpose. And with this new income, I already know what the next question will be: Do I have to pay taxes on this new income? Thought you'd never ask...

NOTES

— CHAPTER FIVE —

UBIT is Not a Four Letter Word!

MAXIMIZING REVENUE DESPITE UBIT

One thing most nonprofits love is their tax-exempt status. But you will find that as you generate non-traditional revenue streams, you may need to adjust your thinking about taxes and cast off your debilitating fear of Uncle Sam. When I encourage nonprofits to pursue nontraditional revenue-generation ventures the most common response I get is resistance to change simply from fear of **UBIT (Unrelated Business Income Tax)**! UBIT is tax a nonprofit has to pay on earned revenue. In order for revenue generated by nonprofits to avoid taxation, that revenue must be justifiable as being relevant to the organization's stated mission. Revenue is subject to UBIT when it fails to meet those criteria.

Wait, don't panic! A nonprofit having to pay taxes on earned revenue is not the end of the world... neither is it a foregone conclusion. I can speak with authority on this subject as this topic was the basis of my MBA thesis entitled: *"A Case Supporting The Tax Exempt Status Of Revenues Generated By Not-For-Profit Fitness Centers."* Here's a short summary of my findings:

During the 1980s, there was a massive resurgence of health consciousness in the United States. Fitness centers had become a tremendously popular and profitable investment and the YMCA was firmly entrenched as the nation's leader in health and wellness programs and facilities. These services were in high demand and consumers were willing to pay market rate for them. The 1980s also witnessed the emergence of private for-profit health clubs, led by the International Health and Racquet Sports Association (IHRSA) who openly contended that the YMCA, due to its tax-exempt status, represented unfair competition to their business. There was definitely a dollar to be made in the 1980s fitness industry; but intense conflict soon arose between for-profits and nonprofits over how that dollar was to be taxed. This conflict eventually reached as high as the U.S. Supreme Court.

The YMCA contended that health and wellness was part of its core mission, and that revenues generated were used to provide financial assistance to low-income and disadvantaged individuals and families, allowing them to participate in YMCA membership and programs. The Y's motto was "No one will be turned away due to inability to pay." The majority of YMCAs were able to retain their tax-exempt status using this position; however some were not. They got caught up in the business of making money, and failed to be able to tie the money back to the organization's charitable mission. As a result, they became subject to Unrelated Business Income Tax.

I have gone a long way around the block to make the following point: *So what, if a nonprofit has to pay UBIT on a successful revenue-generating venture that pays the bills and keeps the organization's doors open?* Do you think the YMCAs that lost what was commonly referred to as the "tax challenge" stopped operating their fitness centers because they had to pay UBIT? Of course not! However, they did get smarter about it. They split off their UBIT-eligible revenue streams and formed for-profit entities to operate them. Further, they ran those entities as true for-profit businesses, taking advantage of all applicable business deductions and loopholes provided by our state and federal tax systems.

MINIMIZING UBIT BY BUILDING WEALTH

Now that you have accepted, or at least considered the possibility, that it is better to earn money that is taxable than to go out of business, let's further explore UBIT.

Nonprofits, like most individual Americans caught unawares by this lousy economy, must now embrace the concept of **building wealth**. This concept is difficult for the masses because we simply were not taught how to handle money in school, or *at home* for that matter. Allow me to be more specific: <u>poor and middle-class families and public schools</u> did not—and still do not—teach young people how to build wealth. They teach them to be employees and consumers, not employers and producers. They encourage young minds to continue to buy into the **40/40/40 Plan** (work 40 hours a week, for 40 years, to retire on 40% of your salary). This plan teaches our kids to study hard in school, graduate from college with a specialized degree, and put that degree to use by working for someone else and making *them* rich. Unfortunately, nonprofit staff often bring that same linear thinking model into mindset of their organizations.

Some call this a "factory mentality." There is more than a little truth to this analogy. If you look closely at our schools and educational system, you will see many similarities to a factory. Bells start, end and divide up the day's activities. The building is divided into specialty areas where a specific skill is taught in a specific way with expectation of a specific result. Students are even divided into shifts (classes) as they work their way through the assembly line to graduation. Nonprofits, however, are no different with their rigid set of rules for what can and cannot be done; and should or should not be done. Once nonprofits have embraced the tenets of entrepreneurship, the next step is to grasp and internalize the concept of wealth building. In fact, failure to do so will all but ensure financial disaster in the current economic reality. Where can nonprofits start this conversion process?

NONPROFITS ARE LIKE MOST PEOPLE

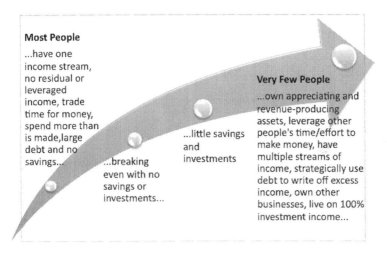

Most People

...have one income stream, no residual or leveraged income, trade time for money, spend more than is made, large debt and no savings...

...breaking even with no savings or investments...

...little savings and investments

Very Few People

...own appreciating and revenue-producing assets, leverage other people's time/effort to make money, have multiple streams of income, strategically use debt to write off excess income, own other businesses, live on 100% investment income...

The above chart, though originally designed to show the financial situation of individuals, can easily be applied to nonprofit organizations as well. The position graphically represented as "Most People" is the one which seems to fit far too many nonprofits today. In the following examples, picture nonprofits in the role of "employee" rather than that of "business owner," because that is how most people are taught to think... and organizations are run by people.

There are two ways to pay taxes in this country: like an employee and like a business. Our tax laws have two completely different sets of rules governing taxation for these groups. Employees subscribe to the 40/40/40 Plan and pay way too much in taxes. Businesses take full advantage of legitimate business deductions, tax loopholes and other benefits afforded them. I encourage nonprofits to establish for-profit entities for their UBIT generating revenue sources, and pay tax like a business owner on that revenue. Why not take advantage of over 450 tax deductions afforded businesses that are not available to everyone else?

Let's look at what happens when an employee and a business owner each earn $10,000. The employee immediately pays, for example, 35% in taxes off the top. He has, in fact, not earned $10,000. He has earned only $6,500! Conversely, a business owner would have full access to his $10,000 for the remainder of the fiscal or calendar year, and would only pay taxes on what is left over after all legitimate business expenses are accounted for. Let's say that he spent $6,500 on his business. He would only pay taxes on the remaining $3,500! If I had learned that growing up, or even as late as college, I would have done things a whole lot differently... and probably could have stayed retired! In summary, an employee is taxed up front on what he earns, and spends what is left over. A business owner spends what he earns first; only then is taxed on what is left over. Nonprofits that know and understand this rule, and make the necessary structural adjustments, need never fear the net effects of having to pay Unrelated Business Income Tax.

However, tax strategies are only part of the wealth-building equation. The next key component is **Debt Reduction**. It is not uncommon for nonprofits to rob Peter to pay Paul. Borrowing money to make payroll many times is a necessary evil for any business, not just nonprofits. Cash flow, or lack thereof, often necessitates making a choice as to which bills get paid this month and/or which vendor is willing to extend collection protocol and accept a partial payment. Tax savings and debt reduction are like two peas in a pod; they go together like peanut butter and jelly, Bonnie and Clyde, Butch Cassidy and the Sundance Kid, Batman and Robin… I think you get the point. Monies saved by reducing taxes can be directly applied to reducing debt. This is where the wealth-building cycle truly begins to take shape.

Reduced taxes and reduced debt allows nonprofits to free up financial resources that can be strategically applied to other fiscal responsibilities; such as deferred building and equipment maintenance, staff compensation, or even beginning an investment portfolio. UBIT doesn't look so scary now, does it? We've eliminated, or at least marginalized, the fear of taxes and can now move on to an overview of the ways in which money will come into your nonprofit.

NOTES

— CHAPTER SIX —

The All-Important "Revenue Mix"

DON'T BE A ONE TRICK PONY

More than perhaps any other factor, understanding the concept of revenue mix is most critical to the fiscal health of a nonprofit organization. You are probably tired of hearing me say that nonprofits don't have expense problems... they have revenue problems. One of the reasons they have revenue problems is that they tend not to diversify their revenue streams. Or worse yet, they rely entirely on one revenue stream like government or foundation grants. Think of your organization's revenue budget as the special Thanksgiving sweet potato pie your mom baked for the family dinner. That pie should be cut into several slices. In a perfect world, the slices would all be the same size;

but, as we all know, this is not a perfect world. Let's say that one of those slices was over half of the entire pie; and that someone got hungry in the middle of the night, raided the refrigerator and ate a piece of the pie… the biggest piece. How do you imagine that would impact Thanksgiving dinner if there was no longer enough desert to go around? Imagine further that if the pie had not been sliced at all, and all of it disappeared overnight. An over-simplification on my part? Of course; but I think you get my point. If the pie had been sliced in many smaller pieces, then one, or two, would not have ruined the meal. A sustainable nonprofit organization requires a revenue mix of significant breadth and depth to survive economic recessions and thrive after economic recovery. Recessions eventually end, and when they do, resourceful nonprofits will be still be around to serve their communities.

Typically, a nonprofit's revenue mix will consist of various combinations of traditional revenue streams such as government, corporate and foundation grants, charitable donations, fee-for-service offerings, space rental, and income from special events. By now you know my feelings regarding over-dependence on grant funding. I harbor similar feelings about relying too heavily on funding provided by agencies like the United Way. At one point during the 1980's, led by YMCAs on the West Coast, more and more Y's began to "fire" the United Way and raise their own money. They found that the restrictions imposed on them were not proportional to the financial reward. In fact during my 30-year career, and never did the United Way's contribution to the Y exceed 3% of total revenue. In layman's terms, it just wasn't worth the hoops that had to be jumped through in order to receive a consistently diminishing source of revenue. Fortunately, we had products and services that could be marketed competitively in the mainstream marketplace; and enabled us to continue to control our own destiny; but we were the exception. Many other nonprofits were not so resourceful.

This is, by far, the shortest chapter in the book... and for good reason. It makes a very specific point to a very specific audience. Before I move on to what I consider to be the bread and butter of nonprofit revenue generation, fundraising and board development, I want to leave you with a working definition of two terms that can ultimately spell financial success for any individual, business or nonprofit: "residual income" and "leveraged income."

RESIDUAL INCOME

Residual income is often described as money earned once, that continues to pay you over and over again with minimal additional time or effort for work you have already done. Residual income is a powerful concept. A good way to internalize residual is to consider its converse context: residual bills. Your utility bill is a residual bill. They only signed you up once, but your bill comes in the mail (or online) every month... without fail. Many of the ways nonprofits raise and earn money are not residual, because they are required to ask the same person for the same thing over and over again.

LEVERAGED INCOME

This is residual income's "kissing cousin;" they make a dynamite one-two punch combination. Leveraged income pays you off of *other* people's time and effort. Many times you will not even personally know the individuals providing funding to your nonprofit due to the very nature of the leverage principle. Sound too good to be true? It isn't. Think about it... when the owner of the company that employs you is out on their yacht, do you think they stop making money? Of course not; they have you, back at the workplace still putting in your time and effort so that they don't have to! There is no reason nonprofits cannot incorporate leveraged income in their revenue mix. A simple example would be investment income.

If nonprofits can effectively combine additional traditional and nontraditional multiple streams of residual and leveraged income, that could only improve their financial viability and translate into being better able to fund the organization's charitable mission in the community. As a nonprofit consultant, I look at it this way. Every nonprofit has both a business side and a charity side. The business side is just as important as the charity side. Before accepting a nonprofit as a consulting client, I always ask a series of questions about their current revenue mix, such as: What percentage of revenue is earned versus contributed? Of the contributed revenue, what percentage comes from government, corporate or foundation grants? Is there a signature fundraising event? Is there a community-based annual giving campaign? What percentage of participants in your special events also contribute to your annual campaign? What percentage of last year's donors gave again this year? The answers to these few select questions will pretty much give me an accurate picture of a nonprofit's fiscal situation. If their revenue mix is not appropriate for their particular type of nonprofit, then financial problems are almost guaranteed. If there is too much dependence on grant funding, it is almost like being on "nonprofit welfare." Too much dependence on money you do not control, money that can be taken from you at any time, or money that can run out and not be renewed… is a recipe for fiscal disaster.

THE VALUE OF AN ANNUAL CAMPAIGN

Since this chapter segues into the remaining chapters on fundraising and board development, I want to conclude it with my personal perspective on what I consider to be the most significant funding source for any nonprofit organization… the Annual Giving Campaign. Please note that I said "most significant" and not "largest." In fact, in many successful nonprofits, the annual campaign is one of the smaller pieces of the revenue mix pie; yet, this does not diminish its value. Some nonprofits subconsciously avoid having an annual campaign because deep-down they sense its potential to showcase organizational deficiencies not ready to be acknowledged. An annual campaign asks community supporters to dig deep into their personal pockets and write a check donating their hard-earned money to your cause. If people are not willing to donate, it simply tells you that your community does not truly value your cause, your organization, or perhaps, they do not perceive the expressed need to exist. Rather than risk facing that potential rejection or realization, many nonprofits choose to forego annual campaigns. This is analogous to someone involved in a serious automobile accident where they have unknowingly lost a limb. The body instinctively shuts down the nerve sensations to the severed limb and subconsciously prevents the victim from looking at the injury; realization of the lost limb would surely lead to shock. The realization that the community does not value your nonprofit's mission and existence is the equivalent of putting the organization into a state of shock.

But on the other hand, lack of support in an annual campaign can tell you where you need to focus your attention. It can help you identify the challenges you face today—and may face tomorrow—if you don't tighten up processes or clearly define your purpose. Look at your percentage of earned revenue and the ratio of taxable to non-taxable revenue while researching your nonprofit's viability. Once you have analyzed your goals, needs, strengths and weaknesses, then move on to that mammoth task of every nonprofit: Fundraising.

NOTES

— CHAPTER SEVEN —

Fundraising...
Keys to Success

PEOPLE GIVE TO PEOPLE, NOT TO CAUSES

A key skill every nonprofit professional must master is the art of fundraising. **Fundraising, to the nonprofit, is the equivalent of marketing in the business world.** Fundraising is an umbrella term that encompasses many other essential skills and techniques. Nonprofit fundraising is made all the more challenging because the great majority of people do not like asking other people for money; in fact, they hate it. And as badly as they hate asking for money... they hate *being* asked for money even more! Be that as it may, nonprofit organizations simply cannot exist without strong and viable fundraising programs. In fact, a nonprofit cannot be officially designated as a "charity" without first proving itself to be a viable fundraising entity through documented receipt of charitable donations from the private sector.

I know first-hand how important it is for a charitable organization to have a strong fundraising infrastructure. Because I managed operating units that generated millions of dollars each year in membership revenue, charitable contributions, sponsorships and special events. My nonprofit consulting company, **G.M. Hopkins & Associates, Inc.**, is located in the Washington, DC metropolitan area -- home to more nonprofit organizations per capita than any region in the country. Fundraising is not just important here... it is a way of life. I would be remiss to begin discussion of the art (and it is an art) of fundraising without mentioning what is, in my humble opinion, its most relevant core principle:

THE PLATINUM RULE OF FUNDRAISING

People don't give to organizations or causes, they give to people; specifically, to people they like, trust, and respect.

This means, that in order to be effective as a fundraiser you must:

1. Be **LIKABLE** -- *able to be liked.*

2. Be **TRUSTWORTHY** -- *worthy of being trusted.*

3. Be **RESPECTABLE** -- *able to be respected.*

Without this basic foundation, it is unlikely that you will be successful as a fundraiser. Great fundraisers instinctively know and implement these principles. Mediocre fundraisers typically do not embody these characteristics and usually self-destruct very early in their careers. However, successful fundraisers also master two equally significant fundraising components: **research** and **donor cultivation**.

1. **Research** is one defining skill required of any successful fundraising organization. Top fundraisers know the donors' wants and needs intimately and understand the critical importance of extensive, painstaking research. They make it their business to find out everything possible about a prospective donor (target market or demographic in business terms), both professionally and personally. They leave no stone unturned in order to gain insight into how much each donor can afford to give... as well as which worthy causes they have supported in the past; and which ones they are most likely to support in the future. You might compare donor research to a lawyer preparing for a big case or a doctor studying prior to a complicated surgery. This process is no less important to the nonprofit professional than the aforementioned examples, or that of the market identification and segmentation process conducted by traditional businesses.

2. **Donor Cultivation or Relationship Marketing** (known as Customer Relations in for-profit businesses) is the process of initiating and fostering a

relationship with a prospective donor, before money even enters the picture. A successful fundraiser is an expert at developing relationships that focus on genuine connections with people.

We can look at a well-known for-profit retailer, Nordstrom's, as an example of excellent customer relations, after which nonprofits would do well to model their donor cultivation processes. Nordstrom's recognizes that maintaining relationships with their customers is much more important than haggling with them over the details of returning an item purchased at the store. In fact, Nordstrom's will allow the return of items *not even purchased at their store* rather than argue with a customer. They gamble that the relationship will bring that customer back again and again to purchase their pricey items… and it seems to be working for them. Any successful fundraiser will immediately see the correlation between great customer service and great donor cultivation.

The quality of your fundraising program is determined by, and is in direct correlation to, the quality of your donor relationships. The steps of preparation described above may be the most important aspects of nonprofit fundraising because they precede the "ask," the point at which the fundraisers actually ask for funds. Successful fundraisers understand that before you ask anyone for money you need to have a relationship in place. Remember, there is no shortage of worthy causes or deserving organizations. Donors often have to choose one charity over another; sometimes making a conscious choice to take allocated funds from one to give to another. Most times, the only difference between who gets the donation and who does not is the depth of the relationship with the fundraising professional who has cultivated the relationship.

No matter the amount, don't assume a donor will simply give you money just because you have a worthy cause. If the only time a donor hears from you is when you ask for money, can you blame them for ducking your calls? This is why prep-work is important. Research your donor to find out what is important to them as a representative, but also as a person. Cultivate the relationship by contacting the donor several times during the year when *not* asking for money. Periodically inform them of how their contribution is being used to benefit others, and of good things your organization is doing in the community. Do this consistently and I guarantee that when you do ask for money—whether they donate or not—they will actually take your call!

STAFF ROLES VERSUS VOLUNTEER ROLES

In order to have an effective, diversified, comprehensive fundraising program a nonprofit *must* develop clearly-defined roles for **volunteers** and **staff** in order to solidify a strong fundraising team. I believe that the only difference between a staff and a volunteer is a paycheck. Both should have job descriptions, performance expectations, incentives, accountabilities and repercussions… but most importantly, each should have signed agreements specifically outlining same. Working with volunteers is an area that many nonprofit professionals struggle with; sometimes because the staff person is uncomfortable being in a position where he works for volunteers. This is the case with many volunteer boards of directors, and can sometimes create a perplexing "Catch-22" situation. The staff works for the volunteers, yet the staff is ultimately responsible for training those same volunteers in how to do their jobs.

Technically, it is the board of directors' responsibility to put policies and procedures in place to renew itself by replacing volunteers as they rotate off the board. In a perfect world, volunteers should recruit and train other volunteers to replace them when their terms are up. However, when they drop the ball, the staff has to pick it up. Of course, nonprofit organizations and their by-laws vary somewhat on interpretation of this issue; therefore, I am speaking generically.

Ironically, one of the main reasons executive directors get fired by their boards is that not enough time was taken by staff and key volunteers to identify, recruit, train and monitor the right kind of volunteers. If the board is filled with "resume builders," fraternity brothers, bowling buddies of existing board members and other people not necessarily bought into the funding and fulfilling the organizations charitable mission, other agendas can take the forefront. If an executive is not careful, stepping on the toes of non-committed volunteers there for the wrong reasons could be a career-ender. These volunteers are like cancer. Once they are in, the only way to remove them is surgically. Trust me, this can get real ugly real fast, and do a lot of damage to the organization and everyone involved. Take heart, there *ARE* ways to get ineffective board members to "fire themselves." This is probably one of the most critical skills for a nonprofit executive to master. Literally, your career could depend on it. We will deal with this in detain in a later chapter.

> "Retaining good volunteers can be a challenge for nonprofits. Yet in order to reap the maximum benefits of using volunteers in your nonprofit, it's important to keep them coming over the long term. If you can maintain a loyal corps of volunteers, your nonprofit can get more done for less money (sometimes substituting for paid staff), create community involvement, and increase your organization's visibility."
>
> –"Nonprofit Volunteers: Top Five Tips to Keep Them Coming", Ilona Bray, J.D., Nolo, Online

BUT WE HIRED YOU TO DO THAT

Another reason nonprofit executives commonly get fired is due to poor performance in fundraising. This would be more understandable if fundraising was supposed to be the primary responsibility of staff. In actuality, fundraising **should** be the primary responsibility of the board volunteers. Why? Because executive staff generally turn over, on average, every three to five years. While this is certainly not an ideal situation for continuity, a more important reason is that the board, not executive staff, has ultimate fiduciary responsibility and accountability for the organization. Additionally, volunteers tend to be more permanent fixtures in a community. When that high powered fundraising executive moves on to greener pastures in a few years, a fundraising program that was overly dependent on staff will quickly collapse. In fact, I feel strongly that one of the worst mistakes any nonprofit can make is to hire someone and put the word "fundraiser" in their title. Fundraising should be everybody's job, and singling out one person will only allow others to take a "hands off" attitude that will absolutely kill your campaigns.

I teach a workshop for nonprofit volunteers and staff entitled **"Whose Job is it, Anyway?"** which drives this point home. The working relationship between volunteers and staff can be a mutually rewarding, or a mutually frustrating, experience if the parameters of those roles are not understood and strictly adhered to. Taking the time for proper orientation and training can go a long way towards alleviating potential problems. Of course, there is much more to being a "great" nonprofit organization than excellent fundraising... but it is a wonderful place to start!

NOTES

— CHAPTER EIGHT —

The Cost of Getting Paid

DIRTY MONEY VS CLEAN MONEY

It is important to understand the different types of fundraising activities, as well as their strengths and weaknesses relative to the goals and objectives of the organization. The "act" of raising money and the "art" of raising money can be quite different things. For example, when most laypeople think of fundraising, they think primarily of **special events** like golf tournaments, road races, raffles, and silent auctions; or the **selling** of wholesale items like candy, donuts, pizza, etc. These are, indeed, common and well-known methods in any community. You can include car washes and bake sales, and selling "quality" dinner or dance time with celebrities. You don't need to know the participants and may never see them again after the event. In these types of event, the nonprofit puts out some sort of incentive to get a donation in return. Many organizations feel this is the easiest way to garner community participation and attention to the cause. I will not deny these methods can bring in funds, but I don't prefer them. These types of activities, depending on how efficiently they are run, generate what I call **"dirty money."** What makes it dirty is all the "stuff" that is stuck to it. Dirty money looks good until you figure in all the direct and indirect staff and volunteer time costs; as well as product "shrinkage" costs.

If a nonprofit organization is diligent about monitoring and evaluating the fiscal performance of its fundraising activities, it may find the money earned at these types of events comes at a high price. Close evaluation may justifiably prompt questions like: How many hours does the staff give to special projects and does it take them away from work they are actually paid to do? How many candy bars are eaten by the staff instead of being sold? Who attended this event and have we done anything to ensure a repeat donor at next year's event? Or even politically-sensitive questions, such as: Why are we paying our volunteer Board member's printing business full retail for event flyers? And how has the board directly contributed to fundraising since—as we know know—fundraising is the job of the board? Yes, dirty money is real money; but it is money that *costs* you money.

Clean money, conversely, supports the **sustainability of the organization** by fostering the development and maintenance of quality relationships; while dirty money builds **no loyalty or connection** with the organization's mission, or to the organization itself. Clean money has no strings attached... nothing "stuck" to it. It is given freely by the donor, and may be used at the discretion of leadership in support of the nonprofit's mission. A perfect example of clean money is an unrestricted charitable donation. The donor simply gives the gift without restriction as to how it is to be used. This is the ultimate in donor confidence in the nonprofit organization receiving the gift. It is like saying that I trust you unquestionably with my hard earned money to do the right thing, and that you will use my gift for its highest and best use in service of the community.

CHANGING "GIVE TO GET" INTO "GIVE TO HELP"

I am somewhat of a staunch traditionalist when it comes to fundraising, and I definitely believe there is an art to doing it well. The "old school" believes the **best** way to raise money is to look a perspective donor in the eye, explain how the donation will be used to further the mission of the organization, and simply ask for an amount representative of that donor's capacity and propensity to give. This "representative amount" can only be determined by proper research... which is the "art" of this process. Your odds for success increase if the donation is in support of a compelling cause or augments a reputable organization that the donor feels strongly about. If you are asking for a **large** gift, you must also have taken the time to cultivate (build a relationship with) the donor, as previously discussed.

Most nonprofits are more comfortable asking others, for example, to buy a couple of $100 raffle tickets for a chance to win a big screen TV rather than asking for $200 to help a disadvantaged teen participate in a workforce development program; or to give an inner city youth the chance to go away to residence camp. On the surface it seems easier to ask for something if you are able to give something tangible in return. Realistic fundraisers acknowledge that there are people who must "get" in order to "give." Actually, this is true of all donors to some degree. This is not necessarily a bad thing. The difference lies in what comprises the "get." In the true spirit of giving, the "get" can be simply a warm feeling of satisfaction that comes from helping another human being. As with most things, however, the truth probably lies somewhere in between.

This lesson was driven home to me quite clearly as a young YMCA program director in Wichita, Kansas back in the early 1980s. One of the most entrenched groups at the Y was a crew of about 20-25 men of varying ages that played basketball around lunch time. Many of them had been members for 20 years or more. Though they were fixtures at the Y, they typically did not participate in member functions or donate to the annual giving campaign which funded our youth financial assistance program. My executive director decided that because I was an active part of that group, I should be able to get them more involved. He challenged me to get $25 donations from each player. Of course, I gave it my best shot, but they had no more trouble saying "no" to me than they did to him or anyone else who had asked. Truthfully, I was a little surprised myself. There was something much deeper going on here. So I did what any naïve young program director would do… I just asked them!

What they told me was not rocket science; but when I thought about it, it made perfect sense to me.

They felt that the Y did not value them as members or acknowledge their loyalty to the organization over the years. They didn't just pay a day fee to participate in "open gym;" they were full-fledged dues paying members! It seemed as if the only time anyone on executive staff talked to them was to ask for something. Even worse, they felt that every other program at the Y was given more consideration than theirs. Whenever a special event was held, their time in the gym was preempted; often with little or no advance warning. Why were the Noon aerobics class participants called and notified of bad weather closings, but not them? But perhaps the greatest indignation of all was that they had to bring their own basketballs to play with. Of course, the Y had basketballs for them; but they were <u>rubber</u> basketballs. No "serious baller" would be caught dead playing with a rubber basketball, so they brought their own...and it really pissed them off!

Now at that point in my life I was not a seasoned fundraiser. In fact, no one hated asking people for money more than I did; but I loved my job and wanted to keep it. So I got creative. Somehow, I instinctively knew how to solve this problem. The first thing I did was talk my boss into getting leather basketballs...piece of cake. This made me an instant rock star. Then, I called in a favor from one of my t-shirt vendor friends and had him design a custom logo for t-shirts that could only be purchased by lunchtime basketball players through me. The logo was very unique with "ELBOWS FOR LUNCH BUNCH" in a bold arc across the chest. Everybody loves to have a nickname, and they loved this one. The shirts were done specially for them. They felt appreciated. They also paid $45 per shirt... proceeds to go to the Financial Assistance Scholarship fund, of course! Now whenever you can convince someone adamantly opposed to giving you $25 to freely give you $45 for a t-shirt that only cost me $5... you know you are on to something. Actually most of the guys bought two or three shirts, and wore them all over town, not just at the Y. In addition to donations, we got walking billboards as a bonus.

The moral of this story in not how to get people to buy overpriced sports gear; instead the moral is that people will give when you hit their hot buttons. Once you put in the time and effort to find out what is important to a person, and develop a relationship, you have a fighting chance to encourage them to become active donors. This opens the door to allowing us the opportunity to cultivate them for future, larger donations... donations made for the "right" reasons. By the way, I raised more money that year than any other program director. Did I mention that they also loved the **sweatshirts** I sold them later that winter... for **$95 each**! Don't be so surprised. After all, I did, decades later, write a book about helping nonprofits make more money! I was merely honing my craft.

The process of giving is very interesting. People give, or do not give, for many different reasons. Foundations are *required* to give. Individuals and corporations get *tax breaks* because they give. When individuals give, they are fulfilling a need within themselves. The idea that some people give and expect absolutely nothing in return is false. It isn't so much whether or not they want or expect something in return, as much as what exactly what it is they want or expect. Wanting something in return is not, in and of itself a bad or selfish thing. Immediately most of us imagine them wanting to see their name in print, or to be recognized publicly for their generosity. However, the need could just as easily be the desire to experience that warm feeling inside from knowing that you helped another human being. Knowing this, there is little need for nonprofits to feel as if they are asking for a hand-out. Instead, they should think of themselves as giving someone the opportunity to feel good about helping someone else. If a nonprofit believes in its purpose it will behave accordingly and effectively employ the "art" of researching and cultivating relationships.

"Donations by individuals are the largest source of charitable giving, historically accounting for between 75and 80 percent of the total."

—"Tax Policy and Charities", October 2011, Urban Institute Center on Nonprofits and Philanthropy, Urban Institute-Brookings Tax Policy Center

NOTES

— CHAPTER 9 —

10 Steps To A Strong Nonprofit

SO YOU'RE A NEW NONPROFIT... NOW WHAT?

Most organizational and operational problems faced by nonprofits could have been cured if caught and addressed early on. If left unresolved, these issues do not go away; they simply become more firmly entrenched and are passed on to future staff and board leadership. My business is helping nonprofits correct these problems. Unfortunately, my phone seldom rings in the early stages when these problems can be more easily addressed. More often, my services are enlisted several years later, after the problems have become institutionalized and are much more difficult to eradicate. This problem is not isolated to the small, poorly resourced nonprofits, but highly prevalent in organizations both large and small.

Board development is key to the long term stability and sustainability for all nonprofits, yet it is often neglected. Even though the nonprofit industry has advanced and become more sophisticated since the early 1980s when I started, today I still see the same basic organizational and structural challenges that I saw then. New nonprofits, especially, often feel that they cannot afford the cost to invest in expert consulting services due to lack of funds. What they fail to realize is what it truly costs them more NOT to invest. Admittedly, this sounds cliché and could be interpreted as being a bit self-serving, but it is true, nonetheless. Take the time to build a sound foundation for your nonprofit organization; one that will withstand the inevitable internal and external challenges that lie ahead.

> *"Consider hiring a consultant when you're facing a key challenge or opportunity or are considering changes to your organization's work/mission/vision. For such challenges, you often need deeper knowledge and an awareness of best practices, as well as counsel that can spark fresh thinking, deliver new solutions, and challenge the organizational status quo."*
> **–"The Sustainable Nonprofit", Derrick Feldmann and David Sternberg, Philanthropy News Digest Online, 2009**

THE BUCK STOPS, WHERE?

Ultimately, the success or failure of your nonprofit depends primarily on the effectiveness of your Board. You can do a lot of things wrong -- and you will -- during the process of starting up a new nonprofit; but if you get Board development right, you can still come out smelling like a rose. When you formed your nonprofit, you had to fill out a lot of tedious paperwork. One of your many tasks was to come up with a few names for board officers and members. The average initial Board usually consists of close friends, spouses, and other relatives ... some who may not even be aware that they actually are on your Board! Very recently, I consulted with a client on this very subject. She told me that her nonprofit was two years old, but that it was still being underwritten entirely by her and her husband. Obviously, this was a huge financial burden on her personally. It took me all of about 30 seconds to diagnose her problem. I asked her how many board members were on the list she submitted to get her 501-c-3 paperwork approved. She said "eight." I asked how many board members she had now. She said "eight." I asked if they were the same eight from her original paperwork submission. She said "yes." Problem identified...

I am sure she had every intention of going back and further developing a viable list of motivated, qualified, and resourceful board volunteers but, somehow, never found the time to do it. As a result, she ended up carrying the entire weight of the organization on her shoulders. Everything depended on her. If she didn't do it, it didn't get done. If it needed to be paid for, she paid for it out of her own pocket. That is no way to run a railroad... or a nonprofit, for that matter. Learn from her, and many others like her; **make** the time to address this issue. I promise you, lack of attention to proper board development will not go away; and no matter how hard you work or how much of your own money you spend, you can't overcome it. Consider it an investment in your organization's future. Consider it the foundation upon which your charitable organization will be built.

Remember, if you don't know where you are going any road will get you there. There was a vision behind the formation of your nonprofit. The direction has been set. Now you have to put the right people "on the bus" to help you get there. New nonprofits rarely have enough resources, initially, to hire a full complement of staff. Volunteer board members are a great remedy for this challenge. Ironically, most board members will probably be more skilled and talented than anyone you would be able to hire on staff... and probably already make more money than you could afford to pay them! So why, then, is the well-trained highly effective, self-monitoring and self-renewing board the rare exception rather than the rule? Opinions vary on this. For my money, I lean toward lack of clear direction, expectation, performance measurement, accountability, recognition and consequences as the culprits. In other words, lack of a solid board development plan.

I came to this epiphany after having to perform one of the most difficult tasks of my professional life... dismissing an entire volunteer board! This was not a decision arrived at lightly, especially since it wasn't entirely the volunteers' fault. They had not been properly recruited, trained, monitored and/or developed to be effective in their roles. No one in a leadership position had sat them down, looked them in the eye and engaged them in the tough conversations about what specifically was expected of them; and of their potential impact on the organization, both positive and negative, resultant upon their actions. While dismissing a board was a difficult thing to do, it was not difficult to see that it needed to be done. Only a very few volunteers were making a personal donation, raising significant dollars in the annual giving campaign, volunteering for special events, serving on a standing board committee and attending a majority of the board meetings. These were key responsibilities incumbent upon every board volunteer. This was their job; and regardless of the circumstances, they simply were not doing it.

The good news here is that once a problem is identified, and the appropriate action is taken; you can move past a negative situation and create a positive one. And, fortunately, we did just that. Beginning with the first new board member recruited, they signed a "board contract" (formal agreement) that clearly outlined in specific detail what was expected of them: the good, the bad and the ugly. These expectations were not optional, and were a requirement of membership. There were accountabilities and repercussions if these duties were not performed; but there was also a rewards and recognition component as well. Rest assured, these expectations were not arbitrarily selected. They were compiled as a result of an independently conducted analysis done of six "recognized successful" organizations similar in size and scope to ours.

In fact, most of the existing board members were not actually dismissed; but voluntarily resigned after measuring themselves against the new expectations. Those that did not resign were exposed as individuals who were on the board for the wrong reasons anyway... and needed to go. To accomplish this with a minimum of hurt feelings and bruised egos, we employed a process called "*plaqueing*." I know it's not a real word. It is a colloquialism, just like "nonprofit." It is an interesting and effective process; but I can't give away all my trade secrets here!

Be purposeful in your board selection process... and just as purposeful in your training, monitoring, measuring and recognizing your board volunteers as well. This is board development at its finest. Don't waste this invaluable resource. Don't take shortcuts. Do it right the first time, and be sure to leave policies, procedures and infrastructure in place to make the job a little easier for the staff and volunteer leadership that follow behind you. If you need an outline on how to do this, try this 10-Step Method that I have found to be extremely effective:

STEP #1: START WITH A STEERING COMMITTEE

Technically, you already have a Board; functionally, you probably do not. Recognize that the initial list of individuals you submitted with your certification paperwork is probably not going to get you where you want to go. Don't be afraid to start over. In fact, if you ***don't*** start over, you will probably live to regret it. A good place to start work on your board development plan is with a Steering Committee, sometimes referred to as an "executive board" or an "executive committee." If you select the right people, this group need not be large to be effective. They do, however, need to be committed to the mission and purpose of the organization. That commitment means being willing to bring their time, talent, and treasure to bear on behalf of your organization. Don't fall into the trap of selecting quantity over quality. You probably will not know all of these people personally. In fact, it is best if you do not. By utilizing your personal network of contacts to identify and recruit movers and shakers you *do not* know; you have successfully expanded your sphere of influence. Congratulations, you are on your way!

STEP #2: IDENTIFY AREAS OF REQUIRED EXPERTISE

Work with your new Steering Committee to identify which factions within the community should be represented on your Board. Initially, concentrate on the "what," not the "who." Do you need someone from the financial community? How about a CEO or senior executive from a local corporation? What about legal representation? Should the faith-based community be represented? Should there be a politician on board? Don't make these decisions by yourself. Get feedback from your carefully-selected brain trust. After all, isn't that why you wanted them in the first place? Just a suggestion ... never allow more than one lawyer, minister, or politician on your Board.

If you have to ask why, then you are not yet ready to leave the temple, Grasshopper!

STEP #3: CREATE BOARD CONTRACTS TO CLARIFY EXPECTATIONS

Everybody should have specific, well-defined, measurable performance expectations. Even volunteers have a right to know exactly what is expected of them, and that they will be held accountable for successful achievement of those expectations. I always had my volunteer Board members sign a "board contract." It asked for their commitment to the mission and purpose of the organization, and to pledge their "time, talent, and treasure" to the cause.

Things can get a little sensitive when you mention treasure. You can't soft sell, or back away from the financial commitment required to be a Board member. Volunteer Board members must accept—as *their primary function*—the responsibility to "fund the organization's mission." In layman's terms, this simply means to give money to and raise money for the organization. Don't move on to "time and talent" until you have a clear understanding of the "treasure" commitment. Trust me, you will save yourself a lot of grief and uncomfortable confrontations later.

> "Board members are not required to know everything about nonprofit management, but they are expected to act prudently and in the best interests of the organization. They approve operating budgets, establish long-term plans, and carry out fundraising activities."
>
> **–"Establishing a Nonprofit Organization", The Foundation Center, Online**

STEP #4: INSPECT WHAT YOU EXPECT

Performance measurement is just as important for volunteers as it is for staff. Setting specific, measurable expectations without following through with evaluation and feedback is a lot like asking your spouse to get dressed up for a night on the town, then canceling at the last minute because you were too busy. Performance evaluation need not be seen as an inconvenience or punitive measure. In fact, it should be an integral part of your organization's *Rewards and Recognition Program* (a program you should create *immediately* if you haven't already). If you stay close to your volunteers, and give them constructive feedback on a regular basis; you greatly increase the probability that they will be successful, and justify rewarding them in ways that are meaningful to them. Remember, volunteers do not get a paycheck; meaningful recognition is what will keep them coming back.

STEP #5: DEVELOP CHECKS AND BALANCES FOR BOARD DEVELOPMENT

Put this process in place early on to prevent having to do so later as a corrective measure. As a staff person, you will have the greatest opportunity to impact the growth and development of your Board in the beginning. The longer you wait, the more difficult and political it will become to influence implementation. You are the expert but the Board is the fiduciary agent for your organization. In other words the Founder/CEO/President/Executive Director works for the Board! If the founder does not put into place the infrastructure for the Board to become self-monitoring, self-renewing, and self-sustaining, it will take on a life of its own that will be shaped by the disparate agendas of incoming Board Chairs who may, or may not, have the long-term best interest of the organization at heart.

This section could be a book unto itself. Here is one suggestion, on the house... install Board term limits. Fish, house guests and Board members all begin to stink after a certain period of time!

> *"Perhaps the most basic responsibility of nonprofit boards is to safeguard the organization's assets and ensure money is spent in intended ways. The most important way they carry out this responsibility is to ensure that adequate financial controls are in place."*
>
> **–"Lessons for Boards from the Nonprofit Overhead Cost Project", The Urban Institute and Indiana University**

STEP #6: IMPLEMENT ACTIVE RELEVENT COMMITTEES

Being on the Board inspires a degree of prestige, but it also carries a certain responsibilities. Carefully screen potential Board prospects to make sure they understand both aspects, and are willing to roll up their sleeves and get to work. Beware of resume-builders who want the title but not the accountability. While every Board Member should give leadership to — or participate on — a committee; one does not have to be on the Board to be a key volunteer for a nonprofit organization. In fact, some organizations require committee participation *prior* to becoming a board member. Committees are where the work of the Board is done. The role of the Board is to assign the work to be done by committees; to approve it, reject it, or send it back for more work. This is because, normally, the Board is too large to perform detailed tasks efficiently. This is the role of committees and task forces.

STEP #7: ASSIGN SPECIFIC FUNDRAISING ROLES TO COMMITTEE CHAIRS

It is important that as your Board members work their way through the officer positions on their way to Board Chair, they be exposed to leadership roles in the fundraising campaign. I strongly suggest that the Vice-Chair be required to serve as Chair of the Fundraising Campaign before becoming Board Chair; and that the Secretary and Treasurer also be given key leadership roles such as "Division Leader" or "Major Gifts

Chair." The kiss of death to a nonprofit is to have a Board Chair who does not understand the details of how to raise money for your particular nonprofit. This process will ensure that the person heading the organization has first-hand experience and demonstrated commitment to funding the organization's mission in the community.

STEP #8: FORM A FUNDRAISING CAMPAIGN COMMITTEE

This vital committee should be the backbone of the nonprofit organization's fundraising strategy. It should be headed by the next person in line to become Board Chair, consist of Board officers in key campaign leadership positions, and include a healthy mix of other Board members and community volunteers. This is an excellent vehicle for introducing new volunteers to the organization, and for screening potential new Board members. You may find that getting volunteers for this committee may be more difficult than the others; for the very reasons we discussed earlier regarding people's prevalent aversion to fundraising. Don't let this discourage you. I always found it helpful to build in service on this committee as a requirement to advance as a board officer. After all, what good is a board officer who can't raise money?

STEP #9: FORM A FINANCE COMMITTEE

You may be wondering why the formation of a Finance Committee is so far down on my list. In many nonprofits, this is the first committee formed. Please do not interpret this to mean that I think it is not critically important to the success of the organization. But in my opinion, if the fundraising program is not fully threshed out and supported, first, the finances are going to be in big trouble. This committee should be headed by the Board member with the most expertise in fiscal management, not necessarily the Treasurer. If you have a banker, CPA, business owner or trustee board chairman on hand, this is the place for them. In fact, the majority of members on this committee probably should not be board members. Like the Fundraising Campaign Committee, this is an excellent vehicle for identifying and vetting prospective new board members.

STEP #10: FORM A NOMINATING COMMITTEE

This, sadly, is probably one of the most underrated committees on any Board of Directors. It lacks the prestige of the Executive or Finance Committees, or the impact and urgency of the Fundraising Campaign Committee – **but it is the most critical committee for ensuring that the Board is maintaining strong leadership and renewing its resources with valuable members**. This is the group that is in charge of updating, implementing, and monitoring the Board Development Plan. In recognition of the importance of this committee to the quality of current and future Board Members, it should be chaired by the Board Chairperson. If, in the future, the organization finds itself with ineffective leadership, this committee has not done its job. At the risk of sounding redundant, this is an excellent vehicle for screening potential new Board members

Hopefully, you will take my 10-Step Method to heart. I guarantee it will help your nonprofit organization get off to a smoother start.

NOTES

Are You Ready To Start Again?

Now that you've got some tools to help you and a new mindset to propel you, take this opportunity to make your nonprofit the best it can be. Go beyond what is expected and ignore those myths and rumors that have been keeping your financials in the red and destroying your hope for the good your nonprofit can do in the community. Donors want to give to organizations that know how to take care of their business properly, and the community will feel safe knowing whatever they give will go into a highly-functioning machine with the ultimate purpose to serve.

Nonprofit <u>does not</u> mean *no* profit. I hope I've made you a believer.

For more information about **G.M Hopkins & Associates** Consulting Services, visit me at http://gmhopkins.info

12639240R00052

Made in the USA
Charleston, SC
18 May 2012